TUTORAIDS

The Instructional Design Library

Volume 20

TUTORAIDS

Sivasailam Thiagarajan
Instructional Alternatives
Bloomington, Indiana

Danny G. Langdon
Series Editor

Educational Technology Publications
Englewood Cliffs, New Jersey 07632

Library of Congress Cataloging in Publication Data

Thiagarajan, Sivasailam.
    Tutoraids.

    (The Instructional design library; v. no. 20)
    Bibliography: p.
    1. Tutors and tutoring. 2. Programmed instruc-
tion. I. Title. II. Series.
LC41.T48   371.39'4   77-25137
ISBN 0-87778-124-9

Printed in the United States of America.

Library of Congress Catalog Card Number:
77-25137.

International Standard Book Number:
0-87778-124-9.

First Printing: February, 1978.

FOREWORD

We can be sure of one thing, and that is that Socrates was in favor of tutoring. After reading the instructional design by Sivasailam Thiagarajan on "Tutoraids," you may well also stand beside Socrates.

There seems to be little doubt that at times we must sit down with students on a direct one-to-one basis. While this is more obvious with, say, the handicapped, it is of importance that we do so with almost any student at one time or another. This need not mean, of course, that it is the teacher from a classroom who should be so engaged. Parents are often involved in "tutoring" their children in both preschool and during school home studies. "Tutoraids," either as a product itself in prepackaged programs for use by tutors with learners or as a procedure to be followed, will be of benefit to all kinds of readers—for, in one way or another, we are all behavioral change agents who at one time or another, or even daily, become tutors. This book will be of benefit to those who produce and use Tutoraids or those who simply want to read and find out how to help their employees learn specific tasks, or their children or students learn specific knowledge and skills. Sivasailam Thiagarajan, as I have said in other books in this series as well as elsewhere, is a skillfull writer who can communicate—and he has done no less in this book.

Danny Langdon
Series Editor

v

PREFACE

For a long time, the direction of technological progress has always been toward bigger scope and increasing mechanization. In recent years, however, people have begun realizing that "small is beautiful." This trend toward intermediate technology has major implications for instructional technology. The design format of the tutoraid represents an attempt at intermediate instructional technology.

My work with tutoraids goes back to my early experience with the educational system of a developing country. But more importantly, I owe a lot to the inspiration of Dr. Douglas G. Ellson of Indiana University, who emphasizes the importance of such technologies in education and has imported innovations from the developing countries to the developed ones. Tutoraids are closely related to Dr. Ellson's instructional design format of programmed tutoring. They both attempt to offer a technology with a human face and to achieve individualization through interaction rather than through solitary confinement.

With grateful thanks to his conceptual clarity and inspiration, I would like to dedicate this book to Dr. Douglas G. Ellson.

S.T.

CONTENTS

ABSTRACT

TUTORAIDS

A tutoraid is a self-contained package for use by non-professional tutors. It contains materials for the learner and performance aids for the tutor. While the tutoraid can be used with any type of learners and for any type of instruction, it is best suited for use in flexible educational situations with beginning learners for achieving basic skills.

The learning material in a typical tutoraid is divided into *lessons* dealing with single instructional objectives. Different *levels* of difficulty make up each lesson. A number of *frames* within each level contain small learning tasks. All frames have the same format and lend themselves to the use of the same tutoring strategy. Tutoring aids specify how to initiate the lesson and how to handle the learner's responses to each frame. Whenever the learner makes an error, the tutor uses a systematic and consistent strategy for providing increasing numbers of prompts until the learner is able to provide the correct response. Other procedures help the tutor decide if the learner is ready for the next level or whether he or she should be recycled through remedial exercises.

The examples in this book illustrate different ways in which this instructional design format helps the learner, the tutor, and the teacher, The format provides consistent techniques for humanistic individualization of instruction. It also provides a validated structure for increasing the reliability and effectiveness of peer, parent, and paraprofessional tutoring. It frees the teacher from dull didactic chores so that he or she can design, evaluate, and continuously improve instruction in the classroom.

TUTORAIDS

I.

OPERATIONAL DESCRIPTION

In this chapter we would like you to watch a demonstration of the use of a tutoraid. After this demonstration we will derive an operational definition of this instructional design format and discuss some of the features of a tutoraid.

A Tutoraid on Simple Addition

Let us watch Sandy Johnson, a young mother, tutoring her five-year-old son, Scott. Sandy is using a tutoraid which consists of a set of 3"x5" "frames," a larger "cue" card with tutoring instructions, and twenty poker chips. The frames are like the flash cards you find in drugstores, arranged in three different colors. Each frame contains an addition problem in large print as follows:

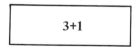

There are 20 frames each of green, yellow, and pink. The problems on the frames all look alike, but on closer inspection you see that the green frames contain easy problems, the yellow ones have problems of medium difficulty, and the pink ones contain the most difficult problems. To be more specific, the sums on the green frames are less than six, yellow frames between five and 10, and pink frames between 10 and 18.

The larger cue card is laminated like the cards you find with emergency instructions in airplanes. One side of the card contains the instructions shown in Figure 1. The other side contains the prompting chart shown in Figure 2.

Sandy begins by shuffling all her green cards. She shows the first one to Scott and says, "Let's play a game. I'll show you a card and ask you 'What's the sum?' and you have to tell me the answer. You see, this one has two plus one. The answer is ... three, that's right." Scott seems delighted, and as soon as his mother shows him the next frame, he shouts out the answer. Sandy keeps pulling out one frame at a time and everything goes smoothly until around the sixth frame, with "3+2," Scott responds with a "Six." Sandy quickly glances are her cue card and follows the instructions below the first diamond ("Correct sum?"). She places three poker chips near the 3 and two others near the 2. She repeats the question, "What's the sum?" Scott hesitates without responding. Sandy follows the next direction in her cue card and combines all the chips into a single pile. Even before she can repeat the question, Scott figures it all out and exclaims, "Five." Sandy says, "Good" and puts the frame aside to start the review pile because Scott had problems with it. She goes on to the next frame and Scott gets hot again. He misses some more frames later. As he gives the correct answer to the last green frame, Sandy counts the number of frames in the review pile. There are three frames in this pile. Since the instructions for review specify five frames as the minimum, Sandy goes on to the yellow cards. The first yellow frame has 4+6 on it, and this stumps Scott. Sandy takes him through the systematic prompting procedure by placing appropriate numbers of

Figure 1

Tutoring Instructions on One Side of Cue Card

GENERAL INSTRUCTIONS

OBJECTIVE

Upon completion of this tutoring lesson, the learner will be able to add any two single-digit numbers (e.g., 3+2, 4+9, and 7+7) correctly.

MATERIALS

1. Tutor's cue card.

2. Frames for the learner. This consists of 60 flashcards, each with an addition problem involving two single-digit numbers. The frames are divided into equal numbers of easy, intermediate, and difficult problems. Green frames contain easy problems, yellow frames contain intermediate ones, and pink frames contain difficult ones.

3. 20 poker chips.

HOW TO BEGIN

Shuffle all frames of the same color together. Begin with the green frames and show them one at a time to the learner and ask him, "What's the sum?" Use the prompting chart if the learner gives an incorrect response.

TWO THINGS TO REMEMBER

1. If the learner makes an error, do not comment or criticize. Follow directions on the prompting chart.

2. Every time the learner gives the correct answer, reinforce him with a "good," "fine," or some other positive comment. Go to the next frame and repeat the same procedure.

(Continued on Next Page)

Figure 1
(Continued)

WHAT TO DO AT THE END OF EACH FRAME

If the learner gives the correct answer the first time through, place the frame in a pile. This is the *pass pile*.

If the learner gives an incorrect answer (or no answer) in the beginning and has to be prompted, place the frame on a separate pile. This is the *review pile*.

WHAT TO DO AT THE END OF EACH LEVEL

After the learner answers the last frame of each color, count the number of frames in the *review* pile.

If there are more than five cards in the review pile, do *not* go to the next level. Take the learner through the cards in the review pile, using the same procedure. Repeat this process as many times as necessary until the learner has given the correct response to all frames without prompting.

If there are five frames or less in the review pile, go to the next higher level of difficulty.

WHAT TO DO AT THE END OF THE LESSON

Do not tutor for more than fifteen minutes during any single session.

After the learner has gone through the pink (difficult) frames successfully, repeat the entire tutoring procedure again.

After the learner has completed the frames for the second time, test him with any ten frames. If he makes more than two errors, repeat the lesson once more.

Figure 2

Prompting Chart on Other Side of Cue Card

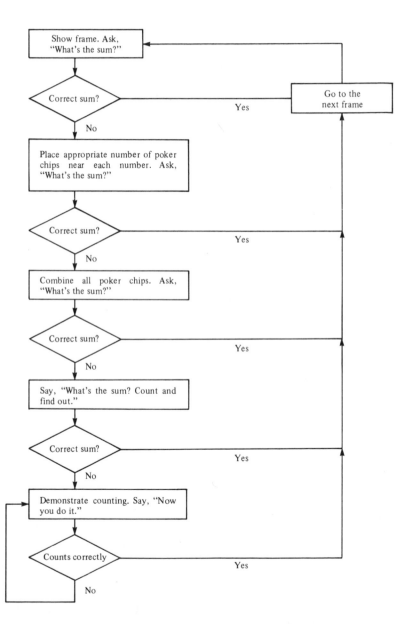

poker chips near each number, combining the chips together, and then suggesting that Scott count. Scott finds the next few frames easy, but in general he has more difficulties with the yellow frames than with the green frames. When he is at the last frame, Sandy discovers that her review pile (frames missed by Scott during his first try) contains nine cards.

Sandy does not go on to the pink frames because the instructions prescribe an immediate review when more than five frames are missed. She collects the three green and the nine yellow frames from the review pile and goes through them with Scott using the same tutoring procedure as before. During this recycling process, Scott misses none of the green frames, but four of the yellow ones. Sandy repeats the review procedure with these four frames and Scott gets them all correct. Sandy checks the time and decided to quit because her tutoring session has already lasted for 14 minutes.

Critical Features of a Tutoraid

Here's a definition of *tutoraid:*

A tutoraid is a self-contained package of tutoring materials for use by tutors with little or no prior training. The package contains learning materials for the learner and performance aids for the tutor. The tutoraid deals with a single prespecified instructional objective.

Let us discuss each of the critical features that are identified in this definition of *tutoraid* and illustrate it with the demonstration we witnessed earlier.

Tutoraids are Self-Contained.

The tutoraid comes with all the necessary materials in a preassembled kit form. Although it would have been fairly easy to require our mother in the demonstration to prepare her own flashcard frames and to use pennies or matches instead of poker chips, we chose to provide her with everything she needs. This is because our experience has shown that the adoption rate of tutoraids is inversely proportional to the amount of local preparation. The amateur volunteer tutors who use this instructional design format prefer fully packaged instruction.

Tutoraids Are for Individual Tutoring.

Although this point may seem obvious, it is worth emphasizing that tutoraids are *not* designed for use with groups of learners. The procedure employed in the demonstration illustrates the need for immediate and undivided attention to the responses of an individual learner. While special types of instructional materials can be prepared for use with small groups in a similar context, they do not come within our definition of *tutoraid*.

Tutoraids Are Designed for Use by Nonprofessionals.

Little or no previous training on tutoring strategies is assumed on the part of our tutors. Like Sandy, tutors using these materials are usually nonprofessional volunteers, teacher aides, parents, and advanced learners in a class. They have no special background experience or expertise in the teaching and learning process. However, this "ignorance" is true only of the *method* of tutoring and not the *content* of the tutoring session. It is assumed that the tutor is sufficiently familiar with the skill being taught in order to discriminate between a correct response and an incorrect one. In the earlier demonstration, Sandy knows the correct answers to the addition problems.

Tutoraids Contain Learning Materials for Learners.

The frames of the demonstration tutoraid are the learning materials. They are structured and sequenced fairly tightly. Sandy also uses poker chips as additional prompting materials for the learner.

Tutoraids Contain Performance Aids for the Tutor.

The cue card in the demonstration tutoraid is an example of the type of performance aid for the tutor. This performance aid permits the use of nonprofessional tutors and yet achieves consistent results from the learners. The tutoring strategy incorporated in the cue card compensates for the lack of training and experience on the part of the tutor. An important part of the performance aid is the prompting chart, which provides necessary and sufficient help to the learners. While the general instructions deal with starting and stopping the tutoring sessions, the prompting chart deals with events which take place during tutoring.

The design of tutoraids borrows heavily from the technique of programmed tutoring as conceived by Dr. Douglas Ellson. The technique of programmed tutoring is perhaps the most stringently validated and successful tutoring technique of all times. A major innovation in this technique is the precise structure provided for the behaviors of the tutor. In tutoraids, this type of programming of tutor performance is incorporated in the cue card. Although at first sight the procedure may suggest mechanical rigidity, very few tutors ever complain of feeling constrained. On the other hand, they enthusiastically endorse the security of being able to efficiently and easily select appropriate actions. An in-depth analysis of the tutoring procedure reveals that far from being rigid, it is extremely responsive to the learner's needs. Each action of the tutor is in direct reaction to what the learner does. This arrangement ensures flexible individualization of the tutoring process.

Tutoraids Deal with Single Prespecified Objectives.

Tutoraids are single-skill packages. For example, the demonstration tutoraid focuses on the learner's ability to correctly add two single-digit numbers. This unique feature is in contrast to commercially available preschool materials which are used in an open-ended fashion to attain a multiplicity of fuzzy goals. Concentrating on a single behavioral objective enables tutoraids to use a single tutoring strategy to handle all of the learning materials. This modest objective also permits brief tutoring sessions which are optimal for both the tutor and the learner.

Variable Features of Tutoraids

While the demonstration was useful in illustrating the critical features of tutoraids, it does not do justice to the divergence of this instructional design format. Some of the variable features of tutoraids are briefly discussed below:

Types of Objectives

The elementary example used in the demonstration may suggest that tutoraids are suitable only for low-level tasks. Although the majority of tutoraids have been written on fundamental, elementary topics, there is no reason to limit tutoraids to drill-and-practice. Some of the tutoraids with which the author is familiar deal with such esoteric topics as creative problem-solving and poetry appreciation. The one major criterion for the selection of an instructional objective for a tutoraid is the need for personal feedback in the learning process. Using a tutoraid in a situation where a self-instructional material can produce equal results at lesser cost is not recommended. Other criteria for suitable objectives for a tutoraid are discussed in the next chapter.

Types of Learners

Contrary to what our demonstration suggests, tutoraids are not always "kid stuff." In one sense, any person who knows less than some other person in some specific area can become the learner in a tutoraid. This makes every human being a potential learner. In reality, however, tutoraid learners are those who are in the initial stage of acquiring *basic* skills in a *fundamental* area of study. Also, these learners are the type that benefit most from a tutoring situation. Handicapped and slow children become ideal learners for tutoraids. However, adults can also benefit from this instructional design format: Tutoraids are useful in functional literacy programs for adults and for providing orientations to new office employees. Adults attempting to learn new hobbies and leisure-time activities are also appropriate consumers for tutoraids.

Types of Tutors

There is a big demand for tutoraids from parents who want to prepare their children for formal education or to provide supplementary instruction at home. These parents are ready and eager, and accept a high degree of control over their tutoring behavior. Other nonprofessional tutors include teacher's aides and volunteer workers in elementary schools. Students themselves can tutor each other with tutoraids. Both cross-age tutoring (where advanced students tutor beginners) and peer tutoring (where students at the "same" level help each other) can benefit from this instructional design format. Other specialized tutors include office workers, native students, and practitioners of various hobbies.

Types of Materials for the Learner

The flashcard frames and the poker chips in the demonstration tutoraid are just one type of learning materials. Other tutoraids involve other types of frames and actual objects or equipment. A tutoraid in reading, for example, may involve a story book. A tutoraid on listening skills for foreign students uses audiotape segments of classroom lectures.

Figure 3

Operational Definition of a Tutoraid

CRITICAL CHARACTERISTICS:

    1. Tutoraids are self-contained packages.

    2. Tutoraids are designed for individual tutoring.

    3. Tutoraids are designed for nonprofessional tutors.

    4. Tutoraids contain learning materials for the learner.

    5. Tutoraids contain performance aids for the tutor.

    6. Tutoraids deal with single prespecified objectives.

VARIABLE CHARACTERISTICS OF TUTORAIDS:

    1. Tutoraids can deal with different types of objectives.

    2. Tutoraids can be used with different types of learners.

    3. Tutoraids can be used by different types of tutors.

    4. Tutoraids contain different types of learning materials.

    5. Tutoraids contain different types of performance aids for the tutor.

The form of the learning material within a tutoraid is usually kept constant, as in the case of the addition-problem frames in our demonstration tutoraid. This ensures the use of the same prompting sequence with different frames. The sequence of the frames usually proceeds from easy to difficult tasks. The demonstration tutoraid uses three levels of difficulty; other tutoraids may have more or less levels.

Type of Performance Aids

The demonstration tutoraid contains a cue card with a set of instructions and a prompting chart. While both components appear in all tutoraids, their physical forms may differ. In some tutoraids, instructions are provided through a small booklet which includes much more information than the cue card. Other tutoraids use an audiotape cassette to provide the initial instructions to the tutor. While this format reduces the amount of reading, it makes it hard for the tutor to refer back to some important piece of information. The prompting chart in our demonstration tutoraid is in the form of "flow-chart" which is extremely functional and easy to refer. The same prompting procedure can be listed in a conventional step-by-step set of instructions in a cook-book style. Decision tables have been used in which the tutor can look up the appropriate prompt for various combinations of learner responses. Several examples of different type of performance aids are to be given later.

A summary of the critical and variable characteristics of tutoraids is given in Figure 3. This figure may be used as an amplified operational definition of the concept of tutoraid.

II.

USE

In theory it is possible to design tutoraids to teach anything to anybody, but in order to attain maximum cost-effectiveness, there are practical constraints which limit this instructional design format to certain specific areas. Here are some content and contexts where tutoraids have been successfully used:

- Homebound and crippled children are trained on self-help skills (e.g., feeding and dressing) by their parents and volunteer aides.
- Foreign students receive training on how to take notes on lectures from local student volunteers during their orientation training.
- Slow readers receive remedial tutoring from paraprofessional tutors.
- Handicapped children receive supplementary instruction on all aspects of reading, writing, and basic arithmetic from teacher aides, volunteers, and high school students.
- Members of a hobby club tutor each other on how to make origami animals and birds.
- Preschool children are tutored by their parents and siblings on basic readiness skills (e.g., recognizing shapes, matching objects, and following simple directions).

- Adult illiterates receive tutorial help on basic reading and writing skills.
- A classroom teacher prepares tutoraids to help peer tutors working on the metric system.
- A group of retired professionals work through a crash course on conversational French prior to a trip to France.
- Students work through cursive writing exercises with help from their parents.

The tutoraid checklist in Figure 4 will help you decide if this instructional design format is applicable to your needs.

All questions in this checklist can be paraphrased into a single question: "Is a tutor really necessary?" Items from the checklist are discussed below to show their relationship to this fundamental question and to each other.

What Type of Instructional Objectives Is Suitable for Tutoraids?

Any instructional objective which requires the learner to respond to a paper-and-pencil test does not need a tutor. A teacher can evaluate such written responses at his or her leisure. With multiple-choice responses, we can use a number of inexpensive "teaching machines" to provide continuous feedback at a higher level of efficiency than a human tutor. However, there are many simple instructional objectives which require a spoken response or an actual performance. Teaching a child to read involves the former, and teaching him or her to tie a shoestring involves the latter. No mechanical devices, not even the most sophisticated computers, can currently cope with these types of learner responses. Instructional objectives which require spoken or performance outcomes thus become prime candidates for tutoraids.

Many instructional objectives permit single-trial learning. These usually involve affective outcomes. Others require re-

Figure 4

Checklist to Determine Suitability of Using Tutoraids

I. **Instructional Objective**

  1. Does the instructional content require personal monitoring of the learner to determine the acceptability of his or her responses?

  2. Does mastery of the skill require a spoken response or actual performance?

  3. Does the objective involve basic skills or concepts which are frequently used in future learning and performance?

  4. Does the objective require repeated practice for mastery?

II. **Learners**

  5. Are there a sufficiently large number of learners who could benefit from the tutoraid on a specific objective?

  6. Are these learners too naive to benefit from self-instruction or group instruction?

III. **Tutors**

  7. Is there a sufficiently large number of motivated tutors?

  8. Do these tutors have sufficient knowledge of the content area to discriminate between correct and incorrect responses?

  9. Are the tutors willing to follow directions and to perform in a consistent fashion?

IV. **Instructional Situation.**

  10. Is there sufficient space and physical facilities for tutoring?

  11. Does the situation permit regular scheduling for learners and tutors?

peated practice for mastery. These objectives are not limited to drill-and-practice items. Many higher-level skills require application and transfer exercises to ensure fluent generalization. Psychomotor skills also fall into the category of instructional objectives for which repeated practice is an essential condition. These types of objectives are extremely suitable for tutoraids, since the tutor can use a single strategy to handle the required repetitions.

While it may be useful to prepare a tutoraid for a learner on some esoteric skill or knowledge, the payoff is hardly worth the effort. In designing tutoraids an important consideration is the utility of the instructional objective. Fundamental skills in reading, writing, and basic arithmetic and frequently-repeated performances in a vocational setting lend themselves to this instructional design format.

What Type of Learners Benefit Most from Tutoraids?

The type of instructional objectives which result in basic and useful outcomes guarantees a large number of learners who will benefit from the tutoraid. Obviously, there are more potential learners at the elementary than at advanced levels. Within these basic areas of instruction, we should carefully select those instructional objectives which are needed by a larger number of learners when other things are equal.

Very often tutoraids are more "expensive" in terms of human resources in comparison with other design formats. Care should be taken to prevent the abuse of this instructional design in situations where a totally self-instructional format can produce comparable results. However, there are many young learners who do not possess sufficient study skills to benefit from self-instruction. These learners may not even have reading skills necessary to follow directions from a programmed manual. They are not always young children; they could be illiterate adults attempting to learn how to read and write for the first time. These "naive" learners can be obvious beneficiaries of tutoraids. Many handicapped learners—the mentally retarded and the learning disabled—form another target group for tutoraids.

What Type of Tutors Can Use Tutoraids?

The availability of volunteer or paid tutors is a major factor in choosing the tutoraid format. Without such tutors, this particular format becomes totally useless. Tutors who use tutoraids fall within a special band of skill level. Using a trained professional teacher or trainer for individual tutoring is a waste of resources. These professionals justifiably feel that they can make better decisions and use better strategies than those prescribed in the prompting charts. As a result, their performance becomes inconsistent and eliminates the major strength of tutoraids. This factor must be kept in mind in anticipating the available number of tutors.

There is a *maximum* limit for professional competency for our tutors, and there is a *minimum* limit for their knowledge and skills in the content area. The tutor should have sufficient reading, writing, arithmetic, or technical skills to decide whether or not the response given by the learner is acceptable. Fortunately, however, the types of fundamental skills which provide optimal instructional objectives for tutoraids also ensure a large number of tutors with this basic level of expertise in the content being taught.

What Situations Are Suitable for the Use of Tutoraids?

Not all instructional situations are set up to support the tutorial mode of instruction. Such formal educational institutions as elementary and high schools are ill-equipped to handle a tutorial program. There is usually insufficient space in which to tutor children, and the hallways and closets are not conducive to intimate instruction. In contrast, the home situation permits more efficient tutoring. Time considerations are equally important in determining the suitability of using tutoraids. A lockstep schedule seldom permits flexible tutoring opportunities. In planning the use of tutoraids, you will have to take into consideration both learner and tutor schedules. While the time period for a tutorial session may be brief, if only a few tutors are available, they are tightly scheduled to derive maximum benefit. This requires that individual learners become available one after the other— a fact which disrupts many traditional classrooms.

Tutoriads are useful in many different areas and situations. However, designing a tutoraid without carefully considering the instructional objective, type of learner, type of tutor, and the instructional situation usually results in frustration and disillusionment.

III.

DESIGN FORMAT

In the first chapter we described and illustrated the critical and variable characteristics of a tutoraid. In this chapter, we shall analyze a tutoraid into its functional components. We shall then discuss each of these components in detail and explain the interrelationships among them through several sample tutoraids.

Basically, the tutoraid is divided into the two major components of learning materials and tutoring materials. The former determines *what* the learner is taught, while the latter specifies *how* the tutor helps; the learner interacts with the learning materials and the tutor facilitates this interaction with the tutoring materials.

The major unit of the learning materials in a tutoraid is the *lesson*. Each tutoraid lesson is divided into a number of *levels* corresponding to the levels of difficulty of the learning task. Within each level, there are a number of *frames*. Corresponding to each of these units of learning materials, there are different types of tutoring materials: procedures for handling the entire lesson, procedures for handling different levels, and procedures for handling individual frames. Interrelationships among these components of a tutoraid are graphically shown in Figure 5. Each component is discussed in detail and illustrated with examples in this chapter.

Figure 5

Components of a Tutoraid

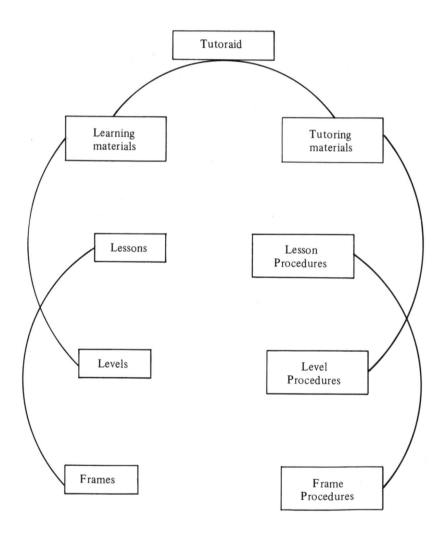

Learning Materials

Lessons

A lesson in a tutoraid is more narrowly defined than conventional lessons. In a tutoraid, a lesson contains materials and methods dealing with a single skill or concept. In other words, each tutoraid lesson has a single instructional objective. This objective is not a complex one subdivided into simpler ones; rather, it is a single "enabling" objective which represents a learning task of an optimal step size for the target learners. The degree of complexity of an objective is relative to any given group of learners. Therefore, the same objective of being able to tell time correctly to the nearest *minute* may be too complex for second graders and too easy for a high school student. An appropriate tutoraid lesson may deal with the objective of telling time correctly to the nearest *hour* at the first grade level, correct to the nearest *five minutes* in the second grade, correct to the nearest *minute* in the third, and correct to the nearest hundredths of a second (from an electronic stop watch) for graduate students in physical education. In addition to being at an optimal level of complexity, the objective for a tutoraid lesson must involve a basic skill which requires repeated practice; and, in its turn, is required repeatedly for acquiring other competencies.

Here are some examples of tutoraid lessons at various levels. For each lesson we have indicated the topic, target learners, and the overall objective. The lessons are from different subject-matter areas; all the objectives involve basic skills in the area which are appropriate for the target learners:

Topic	Target Learners	Objective
Telling time	Second grade	To tell time correctly to the nearest five minutes.
Writing	Adult illiterates	To write the letters of the native language.
Listening comprehension	Students of English as a second language	To answer simple questions about the contents of a segment of a lecture.
Pocket calculators	High School	To perform chain calculations on a hand-held calculator.
Chemical equations	High School	To balance simple chemical equations.

Levels

While a tutoraid lesson deals with a single instructional objective, it may involve different levels of difficulty. The objective of adding two single-digit numbers may be performed at an easy level (e.g., 1+1) or at a difficult level (e.g., 9+7), as you may recall from the demonstration tutoraid in Chapter 1. Not all objectives can be divided into such obvious levels of difficulty. The task of telling time *at the exact hour*, for example, is equally difficult (or easy) irrespective of the actual time. A tutoraid lesson for this objective would contain only one level. Usually, however, tutoraid lessons contain two or more levels of difficulty, as in the following examples:

Tutoraid Lesson	Levels of the Lesson
Telling time (to the nearest five minutes)	1. Tell time when the minute hand is exactly at a number. 2. Tell time when the minute hand is slightly beyond a number.

	3. Tell time when the minute hand is close to the next number.
Writing for adult illiterates	1. Letters composed of straight lines. 2. Letters composed of simple curved lines. 3. Letters involving combinations of straight and curved lines. 4. Most complex letters of the alphabet.
Listening comprehension	1. Easy topics. 2. Topics of medium difficulty. 3. Difficult topics.
Pocket calculators	1. Calculations involving addition and subtraction only. 2. Calculations involving all four operations.
Chemical equations	1. Simple equations. 2. Difficult equations.

As a rule of thumb, any tutoraid lesson which consists of more than five levels of difficulty probably deals with a complex objective which may be divided into two or more optimal ones. Alternately, the lesson may be divided into two lessons dealing with the same objective.

Frames

The frame of a tutoraid lesson, like the frame of programmed instruction material, is the smallest unit of instruction. All frames in a tutoraid lesson have the same format. The tutor should be able to ask the *same* question of the learner and use the *same* set of prompts to assist him or her if necessary.

While the exact nature of the frame may vary, the learner is required to use the same basic operation in coming up with his or her response. Thus, this frame.

```
┌─────────────────────────┐
│                         │
│          3+2            │
│                         │
└─────────────────────────┘
```

and this frame

```
┌──────────────────────────┐
│  John has three apples.  │
│  Mary has five apples.   │
└──────────────────────────┘
```

may be from the same tutoraid lesson (although at different levels of difficulty) since the tutor can ask the same question (What's the sum?) and require the student to use the same process (simple addition of single-digit numbers).

Since tutoraid frames are presented to the learner, they should not contain any directions or instructions for the tutor which may distract or confuse the learner. Unlike the frame in programmed instruction material, the correct answer is not found anywhere in a tutoraid frame. The student receives feedback from his *tutor* and not from the frame.

In many cases, the frame is not the only material provided to the student. You may recall the poker chips from the demonstration tutoraid which are used for providing concrete prompts to the learner. In a pocket calculator tutoraid, the student is provided with his or her own calculator, in addition to the frames on flashcards. Not all tutoraid frames are on flashcards, either. The "frame" of the tutoraid on telling time is a large toy clock. The tutor is instructed to set its hands randomly to create different problems for the learner. The frames of a tutoraid on listening comprehension for students of English as a second language are recorded on audiotape cassettes. Each 30-minute cassette in this tutoraid contains a half dozen five-minute segments of lectures on college-level topics.

An Example of Learning Materials

Let us summarize our discussion of learning materials by describing the tutoraid on telling time. The objective for this tutoraid for the learner is to tell time to the nearest five minutes. Since the tutoraid is to be used near the end of the second-grade school year, its objective is of optimum complexity to the majority of the learners. However, to adjust for individual differences in readiness, there are two other tutoraids, one with the simpler objective of telling time to the nearest hour and the other with the more complex objective of telling time to the nearest minute. The teacher who designed all three tutoraids used the same learning materials so that individual learners do not realize that they are working at a lower or higher level than their peers.

There are three levels of difficulty in this tutoraid lesson. The first level involves telling time to the nearest five minutes when the number of minutes is an exact multiple of five. Examples of this level include 4:05, 3:25, 12:00, and 8:55. The second level involves telling time to the nearest five minutes when the minute hand is on the first or second division beyond a number on the face of the clock. Examples of this level include 4:52, 1:17, 8:42, and 5:02. In each of these cases, the learner is expected to give the time at the earlier five-minute division. The third level involves telling time when the minute hand is on the third or fourth division beyond a number. Examples of this level include 8:59, 3:03, 10:38, and 4:14. In each of these cases, the learner gives the time at the next five-minute division.

The "frame" of the tutoraid consists of a large toy clock with movable hands. At the beginning of each "round," the tutor sets the hands of the clock to indicate a random time at the appropriate level of difficulty. The two hands in this toy clock are synchronized to turn simultaneously as in the real one. The size and shape of the clock very closely resemble those of standard classroom clocks so that the learner may easily transfer his skills to real-life situations.

Tutoring Materials

Tutoring materials serve a very important function in a tutoraid: to produce consistent and effective results from untrained tutors. As we mentioned earlier, these materials program the behavior of tutors and compensate for their lack of experience and expertise. However, the designer may have to settle for something short of the best available stragegy in a trade-off between sophistication and practicality.

Frame Procedures

In contrast to the earlier section on learning materials, we shall begin this section on tutoring materials with a discussion of the procedures for individual frames. We shall then discuss how the tutor handles different levels of difficulty (in Figure 5, Level Procedures) within a lesson and finally the total lesson (Lesson Procedures) itself.

Since the tutoraid lesson is made up of identical frames, the same tutoring strategy is applicable to all frames. Such a single strategy enables the tutor to handle the learner's responses competently without the need for elaborate training; it also provides consistency and continuity to the learner.

Instructions for the tutoring strategy is an essential component of the tutoring materials. These instructions are organized in two parts: the procedure for starting off the learner and the procedure for handling his or her responses. The latter is divided into what to do when the learner gives the correct answer and what to do when he or she does not.

Starting off the Learner

Before a frame can be presented to the learner, it has to be identified. In the demonstration tutoraid, it is a simple procedure to pull out a random frame of the appropriate color and present it to the learner. In the tutoraid on telling time, the tutor has to "create" each individual frame by setting up the hands of the toy clock at the proper level of difficulty. When the frame is presented to the learner, the tutor asks a standard question, such as "What's the sum?" or "Tell me the time." Since this question is to be repeated with all the frames of the lesson, it is precisely and carefully worded. The most important requirements for this initial question is that the learner should have no problem in understanding what he or she is required to do.

Handling the Learner's Correct Response

There are two basic principles in reacting to a correct response given by the learner. The first is to immediately reinforce him; the second is to go to the next frame without any hesitation. Reinforcement is usually (and inexpensively) done with a comment like "Good," or "That's right." Some tutoraids have been designed with instructions to follow each correct response from the learner with a tangible reinforcer in the form of M & M's or tokens. However, such concrete reinforcers are seldom necessary for groups of learners other than handicapped children.

Handling the Learner's Incorrect Response

There are two basic principles in handling a learner's errors. The first is *not* to comment on the mistake or criticize the learner; the second is to go directly to a set of prompts to assist the learner in discovering the correct answer.

These prompts constitute a very important aspect of the tutoraid design format. As you may recall from our demon-

stration tutoraid on simple addition, the tutor uses a
prompting chart which lists the following steps to be
used one after the other until the learner gives the correct
sum:

1. Place appropriate number of poker chips near each
   number to make them more concrete.
2. Combine these poker chips into a single pile to suggest the process of addition.
3. Ask the learner to count the poker chips and find the
   sum.
4. Show the learner how to count and ask him or her to
   repeat your actions.

This series of prompts illustrates a procedure called *brightening*, which has been used very effectively by Ellson in his
programmed tutoring technique. As you can see, these
prompts gradually add more information or simplify the
difficulty level of the task required of the learner. The
brightening procedure enables the tutor to provide as much
prompting as the learner needs without "spoonfeeding" him
or her. If the learner gives a correct response anytime during
the sequence of steps listed above, he or she is immediately
reinforced and taken to the next frame. Thus, the learner is
allowed to discover the correct answer at the optimum level
of difficulty, which is automatically selected for him or her
by the types of responses he or she makes. Also, the brightening procedure guarantees that the learner will provide the
correct response sometime during the sequence, even if only
by imitating the tutor's actions.

Instructions for the tutor on how to work with the individual frames of the tutoraid are usually found on a cue
card such as the one illustrated in our demonstration program (see the frame on page 3 and see also Figure 1). The
cue card is especially designed for quick and easy reference
during the actual tutoring session. While the tutor receives

some "training" on the use of the cue card, he or she is not expected to memorize its contents.

The method for initiating the learner's interaction with the frame is found under the general instructions on the cue card. Here is a sample of the tutoraid on telling time:

HOW TO BEGIN

Turn the toy clock away from the learner so that s/he does not see its face. Set the hands of the clock to show some random time. Make sure that the position of the minute hand corresponds to the appropriate difficulty level. Turn the face of the clock toward the learner and say, "Tell me the time."

The method of handling the learner's responses may be conveniently presented in the form of a flowchart which we call the prompting chart. Tutors are usually apprehensive about the apparent complexity of the prompting chart the first time they see it. However, once the convention of a rectangle for the tutor's behavior and a diamond for the child's behavior are explained, and the system of following the appropriate arrows is demonstrated, tutors realize the utility of the chart. The prompting chart for the tutoraid on telling time is given as Figure 6. As you study the chart, notice the following:

1. All correct responses (whether prompted or not) are followed by reinforcement and the presentation of the next frame.

2. The brightening procedure begins by presenting the task to the child in its most complex form, and proceeds through the following steps:

    a. The tutor reminds the learner that he or she is to look at the position of the long hand and count by fives.

    b. The tutor reminds the learner that he or she is to look for the number closest to the long hand and count by fives.

Figure 6

Prompting Chart from the Tutoraid on Telling Time

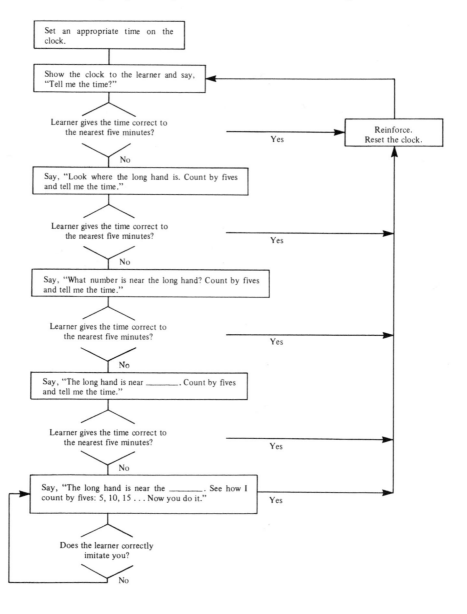

    c. The teacher tells the learner which number is closest to the long hand and asks him or her to count by fives.

    d. The tutor repeats the number which is closest to the long hand and demonstrates counting by fives. The tutor asks the child to repeat this performance.

    e. The tutor tells the time to the learner and asks him or her to repeat it.

3. The brightening sequence stops whenever the learner gives the correct response. He or she receives as much help as wanted, but no unnecessary prompts are given.

4. The chart contains minimum verbiage to permit maximum usage. The tutor does not have to skim through a lot of explanations in order to locate a few lines of instruction. The crisp functional language avoids having the learner wait while the tutor hunts up the proper prompt.

5. The tutoring strategy is reduced to its simplest form. Evidence from Ellson's studies indicate that a single consistent strategy for tutoring works more effectively than an elaborate system of branching tactics.

While we strongly recommend the use of this functional flowchart (Figure 6), to guide the tutor, many designers feel uncomfortable with this format. There are equally effective methods for presenting the prompting sequence. A step-by-step set of instructions in a cookbook style, with clearly readable headings and short sentences, produces effective results. An example of this format is shown as Figure 7. Another alternative format is a decision table as shown as Figure 8.

Level Procedures

Since the frames of the tutoraid are all handled through the same tutoring procedure, different levels of the tutoraid use the same procedure. However, the tutor needs instruc-

Figure 7

Prompting Chart in a Step-by-Step Format

---

1. Give the frame to the learner. (This frame has a model letter and three lines for practice writing.)

2. Say, "Copy this letter on this line." Point to the letter and to the top line.

3. Leave the learner alone while he copies the letter.

4. When the learner brings back his work, check to see if it is acceptable.

5. If the learner's work is acceptable, praise him and give him the next frame.

6. If the learner's work is not acceptable, overmark the errors with a felt pen of a different color.

7. Do not comment on your corrections. Say, "Copy the letter again on this line." Point to the second line.

8. When the learner brings back his work, repeat Steps 4-7. In step 7, point to the bottom line.

9. When the learner completes the bottom line, praise him for his work and give him the next frame. Repeat Steps 1-9.

Figure 8

A Decision Table for Choosing Prompts from a Tutoraid on the Use of the Pocket Calculator

IF THE FRAME HAS A PROBLEM WHICH INVOLVES . . .	AND IF THE LEARNER DOES THIS . . .	THEN YOU DO THIS FIRST . . .	AND FOLLOW UP WITH THIS . . .
addition and subtraction only	• perform the operations correctly		Reinforce and go to the next frame
	• perform the operations in an incorrect sequence		Use prompts in Set A.
	• press (+) or (–) key before the number to be added or subtracted		Use prompts in Set B.
	• press (=) key before the final result	Circle the relevant part of the problem in the frame.	Use prompts in Set C.
all four operations	• perform the operations in an incorrect sequence		Use prompts in Set D.

(Continued on next page)

Figure 8
(Continued)

- press the (+) or (−) key
  before the number to be
  added or subtracted

  Use prompts in Set B.

- press the (×) or (÷) key
  after the number to be
  multiplied or divided

  Use prompts in Set E.

- press the (=) key before
  the final result

  Use prompted in Set C.

- perform the operations
  correctly

  Reinforce and go to the
  next frame.

tions on how to move from one level of difficulty to the next.. The basic factor in this decision is the number of frames missed by the learner in his or her first attempt in a given level. If he or she misses more than the cutoff number, the tutor reviews the same level again. If he or she misses less frames than the cutoff number the tutor moves on the next level.

Sample instructions for moving from one level to the next are shown in Figure 9.

Since the brightening procedure eventually forces the learner to come up with the correct response to each and every frame, no frame is really "missed" by the learner. The frames which are counted as errors are those which receive an *initial* incorrect response or no response from the learner. The cutoff number used to decide whether to review a level or to advance to the next one in this tutoraid is two. This represents an 80 percent rate of initial accuracy. A convenient rule of thumb is to pick a cutoff number between 75 and 90 percent. More than 90 percent accuracy becomes a frustrating criterion even with above-average learners.

The demonstration tutoraid on simple addition recommends a selective review, i.e., a review of only those cards missed by the learner in the previous round. This provides extra practice where it is most needed by the learner.

If there are fewer errors than the cutoff number during the first run through a level, the tutor does not undertake any review. However, these errors are included in the count of errors at the next level. Sooner or later the learner will meet the requirements for all levels. The tutor now decides whether the entire lesson needs a review. This brings us to the tutoring procedures for the lesson.

Lesson Procedures
Instructions to the tutor on how to handle the entire

Figure 9

*Procedure for Moving Across Different Levels
of the Tutoraid on Telling Time*

HOW TO COUNT THE NUMBER OF MISSES

If the learner gives an incorrect answer (or no answer) in this first attempt, count this as a miss. Make a tally mark on a piece of paper to keep track of the number of misses.

WHAT TO DO AT THE END OF EACH LEVEL

After the learner answers the last frame of each level, add up the number of frames he or she missed.

If there are two misses or *less,* proceed to the next higher level of difficulty. If there are no more levels, terminate the lesson.

If there are more than three misses, do *not* proceed to the next level. Review the same level by setting up the hands of the clock to show ten different times and take the learner through each one of them as before. Repeat this review process as many times as needed until the learner misses two or fewer frames.

---

tutoraid lesson specify a number of items. These are listed and illustrated in Figure 10 using relevant sections from the cue card on telling time. Here are some brief coments on various sections of the tutoraid lesson procedure:

1. *Objective.* This section explains the goal of the tutoraid in terms which are meaningful to the tutor; it should not be confused with a comprehensive behavior objective with conditions and criteria which the designer may want to use for his or her own purposes and to communicate with other teachers. There is only one instructional objective for each tutoraid.

2. *What the learner should already know.* This section lists prerequisite competencies the learner should have in order to benefit from the tutoraid. These entry behaviors are listed in behavioral terms so that the teacher or the tutor will have no problem in determining if the learner is ready for the tutoraid.

3. *Materials.* This section lists and briefly explains all the learning and tutoring materials which constitute the tutoraid. This list is used by the tutor to make sure that all materials are available at the beginning of the tutoring session. Any special instructions on the use of the materials (e.g., how to set the hands of the toy clock) are also provided in this section.

4. *Levels of difficulty.* This section provides a preview to the tutor on the number and nature of different levels in the tutoraid. It also provides information about the gradual progression from simple to complex tasks.

5. *Tutoring time.* This section prevents the tutor from attempting to finish the entire tutoraid in a single sitting. Tutoring is such an intensive activity that very few tutors and learners can cope with its demands over an extended period of time. As a rule of thumb, we suggest tutoring sessions of

Figure 10

Tutoring Procedures for Lesson on Telling Time

OBJECTIVE
Upon completion of this tutoraid, the learner will be able to tell time from a standard classroom clock correct to the nearest five minutes.

WHAT SHOULD THE LEARNER ALREADY KNOW?
The learner should be able to:
    1. Read the numbers on a clock.
    2. Discriminate between the hour hand and the minute hand.
    3. Count by fives up to 60.

MATERIALS
    1. Tutor's cue card.
    2. A toy clock in which the hand may be set to show different times. A single knob moves both the minute and the hour hands as in a regular clock.

LEVELS OF DIFFICULTY IN THIS LESSON
    1. *Easy:* In this level, the learner is shown the clock with the minute hand exactly above a given number as in the following examples:
        4:15   11:55   6:10
    2. *Medium:* In this level, the student is shown the clock with the minute hand slightly beyond the number as in the following examples:
        1:42   12:01   3:57
    3. *Hard:* In this level, the learner is shown the clock with the minute hand slightly before a number as in the following examples:
        9:19   2:34   10:19

HOW LONG SHOULD THE LESSON LAST?
Do not tutor for more than 15 minutes during a single lesson.

WHAT TO DO AT THE END OF THE SESSION
If you stopped the lesson in the middle of a level because you ran out of time, begin the next session at the same level. Disregard the performance of the student during the previous session and take him through ten frames at the appropriate level.

(Continued on Next Page)

Figure 10
(Continued)

WHAT TO DO AT THE END OF A LESSON

If the learner has successfully completed all the frames at the hard level, give him a final test: Make up ten frames with the clock showing different times and follow the usual procedure. If he or she makes more than two errors in responding to these ten frames, repeat the entire lesson once again. If he or she makes two or fewer mistakes, tell him or her that the lesson is over and reinforce.

not more than 20 minutes for children and 45 minutes for adults.

6. *Termination rules.* A tutoring session may come to an end either because the allotted time has expired or because a lesson has been completed.

Instructions for handling the end of the session include how to continue the activities during the next session. To eliminate record-keeping chores, the lesson procedure for telling time suggests disregarding the previous number of frames completed by the learner and beginning each session from scratch. In other tutoraids, with larger numbers of frames, a simple system can be used for starting each session from where the previous one left off.

At the end of a tutoraid lesson, the tutor administers a final test. In keeping with the philosophy of tutoraids that teaching and testing should reflect the same objective and assume the same form, this final test procedure is similar to the previous tutoring activities. Actually, the learner does not notice anything different between tutoring and testing procedures. The tutor creates the frames for the test by using a random set of previous frames. In the demonstration tutoraid on simple addition, the tutor picks any ten cards from all three levels. In the time-telling tutoraid, the tutor sets the hands of the clock at ten random times and uses them for the final test. No special instructions are needed for administering the final tests because the tutor uses the same procedure as before. However, a new criterion level is established to decide whether or not the learner "passes" the test. We usually set this standard at the 80 percent accuracy level, but some types of instructional objectives may require a higher standard or tolerate a lower one. The tutor needs to be told what to do on the basis of the learner's test performance. In general, the following alternatives are available:

a. *Completion.* If the learner attains the criterion level of accuracy, he or she has successfully completed the tutoraid. He or she is informed of this fact and praised for the achievement.

b. *Strengthening.* If the learner misses more frames than is acceptable, but provides correct responses to the majority of the frames, he or she is taken through the final level of the tutoraid once again. We may assume that practice with the most difficult frames will help him or her review the skills required by the easier ones.

c. *Remediation.* If the performance of the learner is poor (e.g., if he or she misses the majority of frames in the final test) he or she is recycled through the entire tutoraid, beginning with the first level of difficulty. However, this is an extremely unlikely event because of the individualized tutorial attention given to the learner during the earlier stages of the tutoraid.

A Complete Example

By way of summarizing our discussion of the different elements of a tutoraid, we now present a complete example in this section. As you read the example, pay particular attention to the way in which different elements of a tutoraid are integrated into the total package.

Example: Listening Comprehension for Foreign Students

Many students with English as a second language enroll in the U.S. universities every year. Although these students have considerable reading and writing skills in English, they usually have problems with listening comprehension. This tutoraid is designed to be implemented by local volunteer students to provide assistance to their foreign peers in improving their listening skills.

Learning Materials

The objective for the tutoraid is for the foreign student to listen to a five-minute mini-lecture and to answer a series of oral questions.

Frames

Frames of this tutoraid consist of lectures on audiotapes and questions on a card *to be read by the tutor.* Figure 11 gives an example of the mini-lecture and a set of questions based on its content.

Levels

These frames are arranged in three levels of difficulty. The first level consists of lectures on easy topics with the narrator speaking slowly and clearly. The second level contains lectures on different topics and at a normal rate of delivery. These lectures are recorded under studio conditions to reduce background noise. The third level consists of lectures on technical topics recorded under typical classroom conditions.

Lesson

The entire lesson consists of six cassette tape recordings, two per level. Each cassette contains six mini-lectures.

Tutoring Materials

Tutoring materials for this tutoraid include individual question cards on each mini-lecture. This unique element of this tutoraid contains a transcript of the mini-lecture on one side and the questions on the other to permit all questions and prompts to be presented orally in order to give maximum practice in oral comprehension to the student. The cue card for the tutor is shown in Figures 12 and 13. The prompting procedure is presented in the form of a flowchart in this cue card. The basic brightening step incorporated in this proce-

Figure 11

Partial Typescript of a Mini-lecture and
Three Sample Questions

TEMPERATURE AND PLANT GROWTH

Temperature has an important effect on the growth of plants. If the temperature goes above or below certain critical limits, the plant will die even though there may be plenty of water. These critical temperatures differ from one plant to another. In general, cold-season plants need a shorter range of temperatures than hot-season plants.

The temperature of the soil is often different from the temperature of air. Soil temperature is more critical than the air temperature, since it affects the functioning of the root and the rate of growth of the plant. Farmers control soil temperature by cultivating the ground and irrigating it. Mulching is another common technique for controlling the ground temperature. Just as you can reduce the amount of heat going into the soil, you can also increase it. By placing a layer of black coal dust on the ground, Russian farmers have increased the heat absorption by the soil and have produced mature cotton plants within a shorter period of time.

Frost kills many plants. One way to prevent frost is to heat the area in which plants are grown. But this is an expensive procedure. A cheaper technique is to use a large fan to prevent reduction of temperature near the ground at night. Some farmers add a thin layer of sand to the ground to slow down its cooling. There are many other techniques being tried out experimentally to prevent frost damage to plants.

----

1. What are the two types of critical temperatures for plant growth?
2. Name two ways in which you can control the temperature of the soil.
3. How does a farmer prevent damage by frost?

Figure 12

General Instructions to the Tutor
from the Tutoraid on Listening Comprehension

OBJECTIVE
Upon completion of this tutoraid, the learner will be able to listen to a mini-lecture and answer a series of oral questions based on its content.

WHAT SHOULD THE LEARNER ALREADY KNOW?
The learner should be able to handle the same content and the questions in a written form.

MATERIALS
1. Tutor's cue card.
2. Six audiotape cassettes, each containing six mini-lectures.
3. A question card for each mini-lecture. One side of this card contains the mini-lecture in a printed form. The other side contains five different questions on this content.

LEVELS OF DIFFICULTY
1. *Easy:* The mini-lectures in this level discuss simple topics and use a slow rate of narration.
2. *Medium:* The mini-lectures in this level discuss harder topics and are recorded at the normal rate of delivery.
3. *Hard:* The mini-lectures in this level discuss technical topics and are recorded under classroom conditions with background noise.

There are two cassettes with a total of 12 mini-lectures in each level. The levels are marked on the box.

HOW TO BEGIN
Let the student listen to a mini-lecture. When the lecture ends, read off the first question from the appropriate question card. Follow directions on the prompting chart.

HOW TO CONTINUE
Work through each mini-lecture from the first level to the third level in the sequence in which they are recorded on the audiotape. Use the same tutoring procedure throughout.

SUGGESTED SCHEDULE
Work through three mini-lectures in any given tutoring session. Each tutoring session lasts anywhere from 15 to 30 minutes. You should be able to complete the entire lesson in two to three weeks.

Figure 13

Prompting Chart from the Tutoraid
on Listening Comprehension

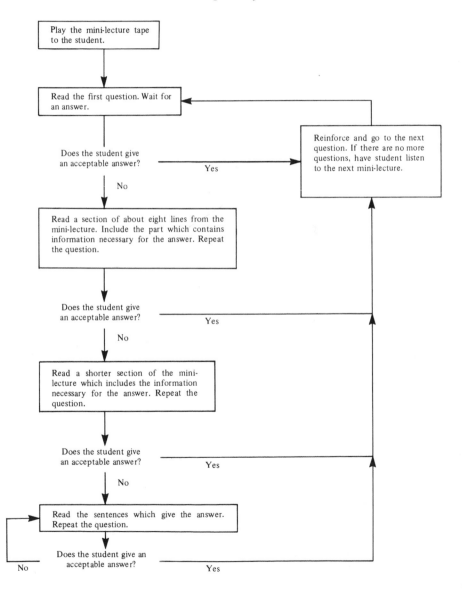

dure requires the tutor to read aloud shorter and shorter pieces of information until the student can given an acceptable answer to each question.

Beyond the Tutoraid Lesson

The sequential hierarchy of tutoraids is shown below:

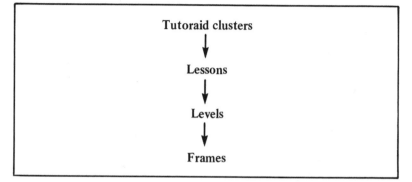

We have already discussed how the frames add up to levels, and different levels constitute the lesson in a tutoraid. A number of related lessons add up to a cluster. Individual lessons in a cluster may sometimes have the same format and use the same tutoring strategy. For example, after the learner completes the lesson on telling time correct to the nearest five minutes, he can move on to another tutoraid lesson on telling time correct to the nearest minute. This new lesson can use the same format (using a toy clock for frames), the same levels of difficulty (easy frames with the minute hand exactly above a division, medium frames with the minute hand beyond a division, and difficult ones with the minute hand just before the next division), and the same strategy (brightening with additional cues). In other situations, the new lesson may be slightly different from the previous ones. A lesson on simple subtraction which follows the lesson on addition may involve the same types of frames but a different prompting procedure. In still other situations, lessons in the same tutoraid cluster may be entirely different from each other. Thus, a lesson on copying letters of the alphabet may be followed by another lesson on writing simple words from dictation. The frames and the strategies of the second tutoraid lesson may be entirely different from the first one.

While the designer of tutoraids may easily come up with a cluster that systematically covers an area of the curriculum, there is no need to do so. The unique advantage of the tutoraid is its flexibility. The designer creates self-contained and short tutoraids to take care of important topics in the curriculum. Coverage of frequently used instructional objectives should definitely take higher priority than comprehensive coverage of a broad curriculum.

IV.

OUTCOMES

In this chapter we discuss the advantages of using tutoraids in formal and informal teaching situations. We explore how tutoraids assist the learner, the tutor, the teacher, and the administrator in achieving a high degree of individualization in the teaching-learning process. We also point out the limitations and disadvantages of this instructional design format.

How Do Tutoraids Help the Learner?

Both the format and the content of tutoraids enable the learner to achieve solid mastery of basic concepts and skills. In terms of immediate payoffs, this results in a reduced number of errors, misconceptions, and failure experiences for the learner. On a longer range perspective, the learner becomes more independent and effective in his studies because of this foundation. An automatic consequence of the improved performance is a better self-image for the learner. With handicapped children, such enhanced performance in the classroom results in more acceptance by peers and a more positive attitude toward school.

Perhaps more important than these outcomes of using tutoraids is the process. Tutoring makes it possible to individualize instruction far beyond the capabilities of any teaching machine or self-instructional system. The tutoraid process provides a consistent experience for the learner. The learner is in complete control of the situation, since each and every move of the tutor is in response to his or her actions. There is no punishment; when the learner makes a mistake, it is never criticized or commented upon. When he or she gives a correct response, it is immediately and effectively reinforced. While tutoraids stress success experiences, they do not reduce the learning task to spoon-feeding. The brightening procedure incorporated in the process ensures constant challenge to the learner. If he or she is not capable of coping with this challenge, the difficulty level is automatically and unobtrusively reduced. The built-in review procedure ensures that the learner returns to face the challenge at a later time until he or she reaches a predetermined criteria of performance. This aspect of the tutoraid makes it a positive and reinforcing educational experience for the learner.

How Do Tutoraids Help the Tutor?

One of the most consistent and intriguing findings from tutoring studies is that the learning gains by the *tutor* often exceed that of the learner. This fact has been recognized from very early times; teaching has been utilized as the best form of learning in tutoring programs. In the process of tutoring another individual, the tutor gains immense insights into the structure of the content that he or she is teaching. These insights become extremely valuable in peer-tutoring situations. Tutoring also provides insights into the nature of the teaching-learning process. There are many scholars who recommend that training of teachers should incorporate at least the experience of tutoring an individual. In this experience many abstract concepts of individualized instruction acquire a concrete meaning. This is especially useful to paraprofessional tutors and teacher aides, many of whom are taking up a career in teaching. In the process of intimate tutoring, the tutor establishes a rapport with the learner. The instructional bond between them becomes a friendship based on the mutual understanding and acceptance of each other's strengths and weaknesses. Many parent tutors report that this intimacy with their children is one of the most positive features of their tutoring experiences.

Tutoring programs thus help peer, paraprofessional, and parent tutors in many different ways. However, many such programs flounder soon after their beginning, with a very high dropout rate. Among the causes for this breakdown are extensive training on the one hand and a total laissez-faire approach on the other. Many tutoring programs treat tutors as if they are "junior teachers," to use an apt label from Ellson. As a consequence, they are taught abstract principles of educational psychology or left to their own devices. These tutors do not have any structured support in terms of useful instructional materials. The use of tutoraids reduces these problems by prepackaging structure and substance into kits. Only minimal training is required to start off the tutor on his or her task, because the cue card provides a performance aid for making appropriate decisions during tutoring.

How Do Tutoraids Help the Teacher?

No teacher argues against individualization of instruction, but most complain about the lack of time and resources to implement a suitable program. The ideal situation for the teacher is a small class size which enables him or her to pay individualized attention to the learners. But economic realities prohibit such a solution. One viable alternative is found in the use of interactive individualization through tutoring. Planning for and implementing a full-scale tutoring program often turns out to be a time-consuming activity. When volunteer tutors perform well, the teacher and his or her learners gain a lot. However, when they perform poorly, the resources required for training the tutors, troubleshooting their problems, and protecting the learner far exceed the payoffs. The use of tutoraids permits the teacher to obtain consistent performance from divergent tutors. The teacher may develop a series of tutoraids as and when the need arises in his or her classroom. He or she can provide simple training to his or her aides or to parents and let them implement the tutoraid program at a mutually convenient schedule. In the use of tutoraids, the teacher is saved from a constant "What do I do now?" syndrome of his or her bewildered tutors.

How Do Administrators Gain from the Use of Tutoraids?

The educational administrator is faced with the increasing cost of hiring teachers and their militant demands for reduced class size. Educational expenditure has been growing dangerously faster than the GNP for the past twenty years. As many economists point out, the only way to avoid a total economic breakdown is to mix "cheaper" people with the trained professional cadre. Fortunately, there is a huge untapped reservoir of volunteers and parents eager to help in the educational endeavor. Parents of educationally disadvantaged children—the group which can benefit most from tutoring—are also those with high educational aspirations for their children. While this increased motivational level acts in the administrator's favor, these parents have neither the time nor the background to undertake complex tutorial responsibilities. Tutoraids can neatly fit in this situation.

Educational research is usually undertaken in laboratory settings, and its outcomes are rarely of any practical value to the administrator in a school system. The use of tutoraids suggests a method for field-based experimentation which is of immediate relevance to schooling. Tutoraids result in consistent human performance and thus control a major source of variance in experiments. Alternative approaches to reading, for example, may be built into a series of tutoraids.

Results from their use over long periods of time will yield findings which are applicable not only to tutoring situations but to many other aspects of mainstream education.

By way of summary, tutoraids use a positive process to provide the learner with achievement gains and a better self image. They enable tutors to gain insights into what they are teaching and how they should be teaching. Teachers find a flexible format for interactive individualization in tutoraids. Administrators can achieve higher cost-effectiveness through their use. Of course, no single instructional design format can provide all the solutions, or be totally free from limitations and disadvantages.

Limitations and Disadvantages of Tutoraids

Tutoraids enable learners to achieve only a limited range of instructional objectives. There are many other higher-level cognitive goals and affective objectives for which the use of tutoraids is inefficient. While some of the author's colleagues have tried this format to achieve such goals as art appreciation and creative thinking, we doubt if such use is justifiable on a long range basis. Tutoraids serve a limited target population very effectively but do not fulfill the needs of others. They are an ideal instructional design format for learners who are handicapped in some fashion. But their use with learners who are capable of independent study is not as cost-effective as many other alternatives. For maximum benefit, the instructional objective for a tutoraid should be an elementary one which is within the repertoire of a large group of peers, parents, and volunteers. Higher-level topics, for which such large numbers of tutors are not available, cannot be sustained through the use of tutoraids on a cost-benefit basis. Finally, there are many willing people who do not have the personality required for consistent use of the tutoring procedure. Creative people feel constrained by the demands of the tutoraid and eventually feel miserable or begin creating their own unvalidated procedures.

Tutoraid as Intermediate Instructional Technology

With all its strengths and weaknesses, tutoraids represent what may be called "intermediate instructional technology." As the economist E. F. Schumacher points out in his book *Small Is Beautiful,* such intermediate technologies are often preferable to large-scale versions because of their less disruptive nature and fewer undesirable side-effects. Tutoraid technology is more modest than the elaborate instructional technologies with computers and costly media hardware. But tutoraids do represent an advance over conventional techniques and are an emerging "technology with a human face." The function of tutoraids, especially in developing nations, may be best described by slightly altering a statement attributed to Mahatma Gandhi: They emphasize education by the masses rather than mass education.

V.

DEVELOPMENTAL GUIDE

By this time you should be familiar with the nature and use of tutoraids. In this chapter we describe a 12-step procedure for developing your own tutoraid. This procedure is given in the checklist below:

CHECKLIST FOR DEVELOPING A TUTORAID
1. Select a suitable instructional objective.
2. Specify the general format for frames.
3. Specify levels of difficulty.
4. Prepare a complete set of frames.
5. Design a tutoring stragety for individual frames.
6. Design a review procedure.
7. Design a termination procedure.
8. Prepare a cue card for tutors.
9. Assemble the tutoraid.
10. Try out the tutoraid with a learner and make suitable revisions.
11. Try out the tutoraid with a tutor and make suitable revisions.
12. Try out the tutoraid in a typical use situation and make suitable revisions.

Each step in this procedure is briefly described below and progressively illustrated with a sample tutoraid on naming letters:

1. *Specify a suitable instructional objective.* This step involves selecting an objective which is suitable for the target learners and requires personal monitoring of the learners' responses. This objective should involve some basic skill which requires repeated practice.

Our sample tutoraid is being developed by Harriet Sheppard, a first-grade teacher. She selects as her objective a preparatory activity for beginning reading—naming different letters of the alphabet. Specifically, her objective calls for the learner to read all *lower-case* letters of the alphabet.

2. *Specify the general format for the frame.* This format depends upon the instructional objective and the type of learners. At this stage, a tentative decision is made about the physical format of the frame and the content presented in each.

From her previous experience, Harriet knows that one of the major problems faced by children is being able to discriminate between such pairs of letters as *b* and *d*. So Harriet decides to present the learner with pairs of lower-case letters on individual flash cards. The general format she has selected looks like this:

3. *Specify levels of difficulty.* In this step, the content of the lesson is divided into a number of levels of difficulty. Usually a tutoraid lesson consists of two to five such levels.

Harriet knows that the "b-d" pair is more difficult for her learners to read than the "a-b" pair. In order to define her levels in more general terms, Harriet divides all lower case letters into "straight" letters and "curved" ones. There are nine straight ones (i, k, l, t, v, w, x, y, and z) by her definition and 17 curved ones. Harriet defines her five levels of difficulty in the following fashion:

Level 1. This consists of the same letter appearing twice.

Level 2. This consists of pairs of different letters, one of which is straight and the other curved.

Level 3. This consists of pairs of different letters, both of which are straight.

Level 4. This consists of pairs of different letters, both of which are curved.

Level 5. This consists of frequently confused pairs of letters.

4. *Prepare a complete set of frames.* In this step, the required number of frames for each level are produced. Actual production may range all the way from local production in a teacher's classroom to professional preparation in a print shop.

Harriet uses inexpensive 3 x 5 cards and a felt pen for her production activity. She creates 15 pairs of letters for her first level, using the 15 on which her children need extra practice. For the second level, each of the nine straight letters appears at least once, with six of them being repeated and paired with a different curved letter. For her third level, she pairs each of the nine straight letters with some other letter and adds some extra combinations. She makes sure that the same two letters are not paired more than once. She uses a similar system for her fourth level. Her final level contains eight pairs of similar letters appearing in two different orders. Harriet uses a different colored card for each level to simplify sorting them out.

5. *Design a tutoring strategy for individual frames.* This step involves working out a sequence of brightening steps which reduce the difficulty level of the learning task by adding more information and providing prompts.

Harriet's brightening sequence consists of these steps:

1. The learner is required to read the pair of letters.

2. The learner is told the name of one letter and asked to read the other letter.

3. The learner is told the name of both letters and asked to repeat them.

This is a fairly simple and direct sequence which concludes with a simple repetition task.

6. *Design a review procedure.* This procedure specifies what to do with the frames which are missed by the learner during his or her first attempt. It also tells the tutor how to proceed from one level to the next.

Harriet decides to have all the missed frames reviewed at the end of each level. This procedure is repeated until the learner gives the correct response to all frames in that level. When this happens, the tutor proceeds to the next higher level.

7. *Design a termination procedure.* In this step instructions for the completion of the final level are specified. This usually involves a final testing procedure and criteria for successful performance by the learner.

Harriet's final test is an easy one to assemble and to administer. The tutor merely pulls out ten random cards, two from each level, and presents them to the learner as before. The learner has to read the letters on at least nine cards without any prompts to pass the test. If he or she does not pass the test, the final two levels of the lesson are reviewed once more.

8. *Prepare a cue card for the tutor.* In this step, the tutoring materials are prepared. This is usually in the form of a cue card which contains a set of general instructions and a description of the prompting procedure.

Harriet's cue card is shown in Figure 14. Since the prompting procedure is an extremely simple one, she incorporates it with the general instructions.

Figure 14

Cue Card from Tutoraid on Reading Lower-Case Letters

OBJECTIVE
Upon completion of this tutoraid, the learner will read all lower-case letters of the alphabet presented two at a time.

MATERIALS
An instruction card for the tutor and 80 flashcards with pairs of letters. These cards are called *frames.*

LEVELS OF DIFFICULTY
There are five levels of difficulty among the frames. The first level consists of pairs of identical letters and the last one consists of pairs of easily confused letters. The levels are arranged according to an increasing order of difficulty in these colors: white, green, yellow, pink, and blue.

HOW TO BEGIN
Pull a card from the white level and show it to the learner. Say, "Read these two letters."

WHAT TO DO WHEN THE LEARNER GIVES THE CORRECT ANSWER.
Immediately praise the learner. Proceed to the next frame.

WHAT TO DO WHEN THE LEARNER DOES NOT GIVE THE CORRECT ANSWER.
Do not comment on the mistake. Read the first letter and ask the learner to read the other letter.
If he still does not give the correct answer, read both letters and ask the learner to repeat them.
Keep the frames in which the learner makes a mistake in a separate review pile.

WHAT TO DO AT THE END OF EACH LEVEL
Work through the cards in the review pile. Use the same procedure as before and repeat the process until the learner has read all pairs of letters correctly in his first attempt.
Proceed to the next level of difficulty.

WHAT TO DO AT THE END OF THE LESSON
When the learner has successfully completed the final level, remove two frames of each color. Present them to the learner one frame at a time. If the learner reads less than eight cards, review the last two levels.

9. *Assemble the tutoraid.* This step involves putting together the learning and tutoring materials.

Harriet gets her flashcard frames and her cue card together. She double-checks the instructions on the cue card to make sure that they fit the frames.

10. *Try out the tutoraid with a learner and make suitable revisions.* This is the first of the three developmental testing and revision steps. In this step, the developer of the tutoraid tries out his or her learning materials and the cue card on a few representative learners. During the process, the developer makes sure that he or she faithfully follows the instructions on the cue card. If the tryout reveals the need for any changes in the frames or in the tutoring procedure, they are carefully incorporated in the tutoraid.

Harriet's first test session is rough. The child she picked has problems reading many of the letters. Harriet increases the number of frames in the first level to 26 to cover all letters of the alphabet. During her second tryout Harriet notices that her new learner has particular problems in discriminating between *c* and *e*. She adds this pair to her final level of difficulty.

11. *Try out the tutoraid with a tutor and make suitable revisions.* In this second installment of evaluation and revision, the developer has a representative tutor use the tutoraid. The developer plays the role of a learner and takes the tutor through various types of responses to test the adequacy of the tutoring procedure. Any changes suggested by this tryout are incorporated in the tutoring materials.

Since this tutoraid is designed for use by parents, Harriet has a couple of parents of the children in the classroom practice working through it. She plays the role of a slow learner and takes each of her tutors through all combinations of responses. In general, the tutors are able to follow the prompting procedure without any difficulty. But, both tutors start prompting very rapidly. To reduce their impatience, Harriet adds a line to the cue card to stress the need to pause for at least five seconds before beginning the prompting sequence.

12. *Try out the tutoraid in a typical-use situation and make suitable revisions.* During this final evaluation step, the developer observes a representative tutor working through the tutoraid with a learner. On the basis of feedback from this type of testing, final revisions are made.

Harriet's final evaluation does not reveal any major problems. However, on the basis of the tutor's suggestion, she simplifies some of the instructions in the cue card. On the basis of the learner's suggestion, she increases the size of the letters on the frames.

In this chapter we reviewed earlier discussions from the point of view of the developmental sequence. The one new concept introduced in this chapter is that of systematic evaluation and revision of the tutoraid. Although this concept has received only scant attention in this book, it is an extremely important one in the successful design and use of tutoraids. Through repeated tryouts and revisions, not only the tutoraid but also its developer become more effective and efficient.

VI.

RESOURCES

Tutoraids are such relative newcomers to the instructional design field that there are very few additional references which directly discuss this format. The following articles by the author contain information on different aspects of tutoring:

- Humans Rediscovered: No, There Won't be a Teacher Shortage in the Year 2000. In J. G. Sherman (Ed.) *Forty-one Germinal Papers: A Selection of Readings on the Keller Plan.* Menlo Park, California: W. A. Benjamin, 1974.
- Madras System Revisited: A New Structure for Peer Tutoring. *Educational Technology,* 1973, *13*(12), 10-13.
- Exceptional Children, unexceptional grown-ups and mediated resources. *Audiovisual Instruction,* 1973, *18*(2), 21-22.
- Programming Tutorial Behavior: Another Application of the Programing Process. *Improving Human Performance: A Research Quarterly,* 1972, *1*(2), 5-16.

VII.

APPENDIX

ADDITIONAL EXAMPLES OF TUTORAIDS

This appendix contains five sample tutoraids prepared by participants in a recent workshop in which this book was field tested. These examples deal with the diverse topics of Japanese paper folding, Indian Yogic exercises, Tamil letters of the alphabet, Spanish conversation phrases, and technical review of a film. The description of each tutoraid includes brief background notes, an edited version of the tutor's cue card, and the prompting chart. The background notes indicate who the target learners and tutors are and provides a rationale for the selection of the tutoraid format. This description also analyzes the nature of the frames presented to the learner and the steps in the brightening process used by the tutor. The tutor's cue card contains a description of the learning materials and the tutoring procedure. All prompting charts are in the flowchart format, retaining the original choice of the workshop participants.

These tutoraids are not ideal examples, but rather samples of prototype materials produced by the users of an earlier version of this book. It will be an interesting and instructional exercise for the reader to critique each tutoraid (using such checklists as the one found on page 17) and to revise it to improve its effectiveness.

1. ORIGAMI

This tutoraid is designed to help adults and children learn Japanese paper folding (origami) techniques to create various animal and bird shapes. Origami is an interesting and inexpensive hobby which can be practised by anyone who has a sheet of paper. Many excellent books on origami provide step-by-step diagrams for folding various shapes. However, the symbols and conventions used in these diagrams are fairly difficult to understand. Personal demonstration and feedback are perhaps the most effective techniques for helping the new origamist translate nonverbal instructions to proper folds on the paper. Many enthusiastic origamists are available to provide tutorial help to these beginners.

The frames of this tutoraid are diagrams from standard origami books which are printed on one or two pages showing the gradual transition of a piece of paper through a number of folds to a specific origami shape. The frames are arranged into two levels of difficulty: Easy ones which involve a basic square form with simple symbols, and difficult ones which involve more complex basic forms with more complicated symbols.

Here are the steps in the brightening procedure used for prompting the learner in this tutoraid:

1. The learner is asked to study the diagram and re-do the fold in which he made an error.

2. The tutor explains specific features of the diagram and asks the learner to re-do the fold.

3. The tutor demonstrates the fold and asks the learner to repeat the fold.

ORIGAMI: TUTOR'S CUE CARD

OBJECTIVE

Upon completion of this tutoring experience, the learner will independently follow origami diagrams and fold specific shapes without any error.

MATERIALS

1. Tutor's cue card.
2. Twelve sample origami diagrams.
3. Square pieces of paper.

LEVELS OF DIFFICULTY

1. *Easy*: Six of the diagrams involve the basic square form and use simple symbols for peak and valley folds.

2. *Difficult*: The other six diagrams involve more complex basic forms and use symbols for folding over, tucking in, etc.

HOW TO BEGIN

Give the learner a square piece of paper and the appropriate origami diagram. Ask him to fold the paper, one step at a time, following individual diagrams. Watch the learner as he makes his folds.

HOW TO CONTINUE

If the learner makes a mistake, or asks for help, use the prompting chart.

HOW TO TERMINATE

Continue the session until the learner has completed at least one origami figure.

HOW TO RECYCLE

If the learner needed your help more than five times, have him repeat the same origami shape.

If the learner needed your help more than twice but less than six times, go to another origami shape at the same level of difficulty.

If the learner needed your help less than three times, go to another origami shape at the more difficult level. If he is already at this level, the learner is ready to work independently.

ORIGAMI: PROMPTING CHART

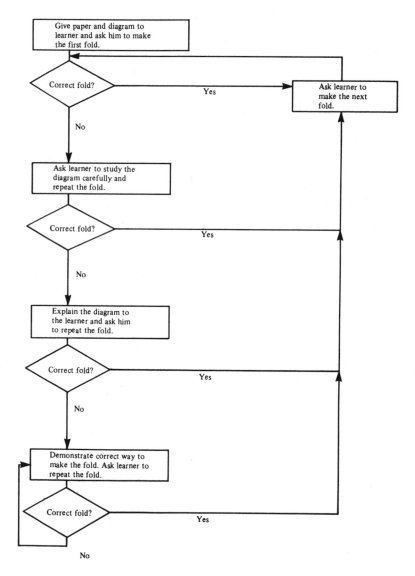

2. YOGIC POSTURES

This tutoraid was created for members of a neighborhood exercise group where the single trainer was unable to cope with the demand for personal attention from many learners. Since the instructional content involved various psychomotoric activities which required personal demonstration and correction and since the teacher had a number of advanced students, he chose the tutoring format. However, all tutoring sessions are held in a large auditorium under his supervision. Because of the slight element of physical risk involved, there is a special precaution on the tutor's cue card.

The "frames" of this tutoraid are actual demonstrations by the tutor. The trainee is asked to watch this demonstration and to imitate it. The steps in the brightening sequence are given below:

1. Tutor demonstrates the posture and returns to normal sitting position. Trainee is asked to imitate what the tutor did.

2. Tutor demonstrates the posture and retains it. Trainee is asked to imitate the tutor's moves and end up with the present posture.

3. Tutor demonstrates the posture, one step at a time. Trainee is asked to imitate each step until he achieves the final posture.

YOGIC POSTURES: CUE CARD

OBJECTIVE
Upon completion of this tutoring experience, the trainee will correctly demonstrate all of the 12 basic yogic postures.

MATERIAL
Tutor's cue card.

SEQUENCE OF INSTRUCTION
Although the twelve postures are arranged in an approximate order of increasing difficulty, individual learners may have more problems with some of the earlier ones than the latter ones. However, it is important that the postures be mastered in the given order.

HOW TO BEGIN
Demonstrate the first posture, talking to the trainee as you do so, pointing out special moves and precautions. Retain the posture for a few minutes and let the trainee study it. Return to your normal sitting or standing position and ask the trainee to do what you demonstrated.

HOW TO CONTINUE
Use the prompting chart to assist the trainee if necessary.

HOW TO TERMINATE
Do not teach more than two postures during any session. After the second one, recycle through either or both postures, if you had to prompt the trainee earlier. Continue the session until the learner is able to achieve the postures without any prompts.

CAUTION
It is possible that your trainee may get himself into some awkward position without being able to untangle himself. If this happens, and/or if the trainee complains of any pain during the session, do not attempt to help him. Report immediately to the supervising trainer.

YOGIC POSTURES: PROMPTING CHART

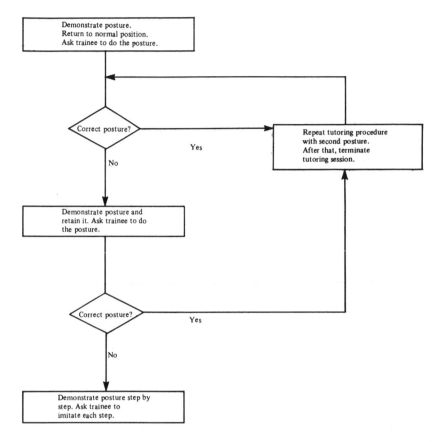

3. COPYING TAMIL LETTERS

This tutoraid is used in an adult literacy program to teach villagers how to write the letters of the Tamil language. While there are some regular patterns among the 246 letters (which include not only vowels and consonants but also consonant-vowel combinations), there are so many exceptions that each letter has to be taught individually. The object of this tutoraid is not to write letters from dictation, but merely to copy specific letters.

The tutors for this program come from different backgrounds: high school dropouts, housewives, primary school teachers, and social workers. To conserve paper, the learning materials are created on the spot by the tutors on a reusable slate. Each frame consists of an appropriate letter to be copied with a blank line below the letter. The first three groups of frames deal with thirty letters representing pure vowels and consonants. They are arranged in three groups of increasing difficulty. The next 18 groups deal with consonant-vowel combinations, each set having the same base consonant.

The tutor and the villager use slate-pencils of different colors. The brightening procedure consists of these three steps:

1. Erasing the villager's letter and asking him to copy again.
2. Overmaking the incorrect part of the villager's letter and asking him to copy again.
3. Asking the villager's to trace the letter instead of copying it.

COPYING TAMIL LETTERS: CUE CARD

OBJECTIVE
Upon completion of this tutoring experience, the villager will correctly copy any Tamil letter.

MATERIALS
1. A piece of slate with the letter to be copied and a blank line beneath it.
2. Slate-pencils of two different colors.
3. Tutor's cue card.

LEVELS OF INSTRUCTION
Easy: Ten letters made up of a few straight lines (e.g., ப)
Medium: Ten letters made up of a few curved lines (e.g., ω)
Difficult: Ten letters made up of complex combinations (e.g., ஜ)
Advanced: 18 sets of consonant-vowel combinations.

PRELIMINARY ACTIVITY
Before the tutoring session, select a letter from the appropriate level of difficulty. Write it legibly on the slate and draw a blank line below it.

HOW TO BEGIN
Give the slate with your letter to the villager. Name the letter and ask him to copy it on the blank line.

HOW TO CONTINUE
Follow direction in the prompting chart.

HOW TO TERMINATE
After the person has copied all the letters from a given difficulty level, recycle those letters which he had to correct more than once. Then move to the next level of difficulty.

COPYING TAMIL LETTERS: PROMPTING CHART

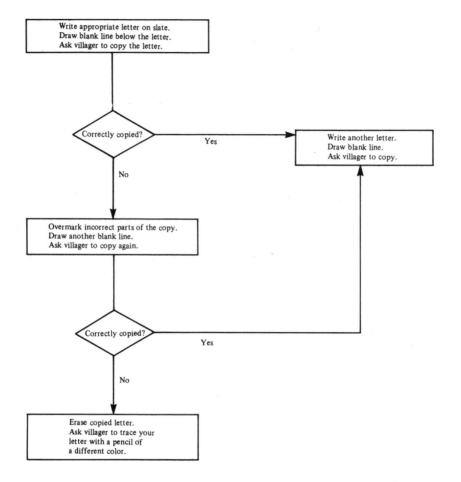

4. HOW TO READ SPANISH SENTENCES

This tutoraid is designed to assist those who need help with their "Where-can-I-cash-a-traveler's-check?" tourist Spanish. It is also designed to accompany a traveler's phrase book which contains English sentences on one column and the Spanish equivalents on the other. The tutoraid does not teach the traveler how to speak Spanish but merely to read Spanish equivalents from the phrase book so that the natives could understand the sentence. Since the tutors are native speakers of Spanish, they can provide a model for correct pronunciation.

The "frames" of this tutoraid are the English sentence Spanish equivalent pairs. These sentences are arranged in ten logical groups related to the activities of greetings and introduction, travel and transportation, arrival, hotel accommodation, eating out, banking, shopping, entertainment, and special occassions.

The brightening sequence used in this tutoraid involves the following steps:

1. Tutor reads the English sentences and the traveler reads the Spanish equivalent.
2. Tutor reads the Spanish equivalent and the traveler repeats it.
3. Tutor helps with specific words and the traveler reads the Spanish sentence correctly.

HOW TO READ SPANISH SENTENCES: CUE CARD

OBJECTIVE

The traveler will correctly read the Spanish equivalents of any English sentence found in the phrase book.

MATERIALS

1. A phrase book with English sentences on one column and corresponding Spanish equivalents on the other column.
2. Tutor's cue card.

HOW TO BEGIN

Always begin the tutoring session with the first sentence from the unit. Read the English sentence from your copy of the phrase book and ask the traveler to read the Spanish equivalent.

HOW TO CONTINUE

Listen carefully while the traveler reads the Spanish sentence. Use the prompting chart to correct him or to confirm his performance. Make a note of those sentences which you prompted.

HOW TO TERMINATE

Do not work on more than one unit during a tutoring session. At the end of the unit, check your notes and repeat those sentences which had to be prompted. Continue the tutoring procedure until the traveler has read all the Spanish sentences correctly without any prompts. Go back to the beginning and have the traveler read all Spanish sentences in the given sequence.

After the traveler completes his tenth unit, give him any general advice you may have about his mispronunciation patterns.

HOW TO READ SPANISH SENTENCES: PROMPTING CHART

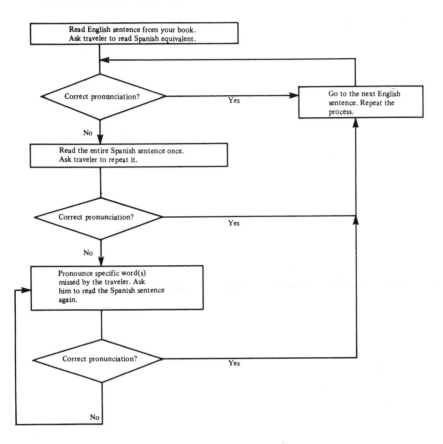

Read English sentence from your book.
Ask traveler to read Spanish equivalent.

Correct pronunciation?

Yes

Go to the next English
sentence. Repeat the
process.

No

Read the entire Spanish sentence once.
Ask traveler to repeat it.

Correct pronunciation?

Yes

No

Pronounce specific word(s)
missed by the traveler. Ask
him to read the Spanish sentence
again.

Correct pronunciation?

Yes

No

5. TECHNICAL REVIEW OF A FILM

This tutoraid is used as part of a film production course where the initial module deals with the technical review of locally produced films. If the trainee can critique other people's films, it was felt that he will be able to avoid some of the mistakes in his own production. Initial instruction in this module consists of explaining and illustrating different types of technical flaws (e.g., jump cuts) in film production. Since trainees have problems transferring from these examples to new ones, this tutoraid session is introduced. Tutors for this session are experienced film reviewers.

The learning material for this tutoraid is a locally-produced film of the trainee's own choice. This self-selection permits review of a film of the genre which the trainee is interested in producing for himself. The tutor previews the film and creates "frames" by noting down major and minor technical flaws.

The brightening sequence used in this tutoraid consists of the following steps:

1. Trainee is required to stop the film and discuss the technical flaw he has spotted.
2. The tutor reruns the film and asks the trainee to spot an unspecified technical flaw.
3. The tutor reruns the film and asks the trainee to spot a specific type of technical flaw.
4. The tutor explains the type of technical flaw in some detail and reruns the film. The trainee is required to spot the technical flaw.

TECHNICAL REVIEW OF A FILM: CUE CARD

OBJECTIVE

Upon completion of this tutoring experience, the trainee will recognize and label technical flaws in a film of his own choice.

MATERIALS

1. Tutor's cue card.
2. A student-produced film from previous years, selected by the trainee. This film should be of at least 15 minutes duration but not longer than 30 minutes.
3. Projection equipment.

PRELIMINARY ACTIVITIES

Before the tutoring session, the tutor should preview the film and note down the approximate locations and types of major and minor technical flaws.

HOW TO BEGIN

Assist the trainee to thread the film and run it. Ask the trainee to stop the film any time he sees a technical flaw and to discuss the flaw.

HOW TO CONTINUE

If the trainee does not stop the film after a reasonable period of time past a technical flaw, stop the film and use the prompting chart.

HOW TO TERMINATE

After working through the film once, check the number of minor and major flaws missed by the trainee. If the trainee missed more than three major flaws, ask him to choose another film for another tutorial session. If he missed less than four major flaws but more than four minor flaws, rerun the same film and ask the trainee to focus on the minor flaws. If he missed none of the major flaws and less than five minor flaws, terminate the lesson.

TECHNICAL REVIEW OF A FILM: PROMPTING CHART

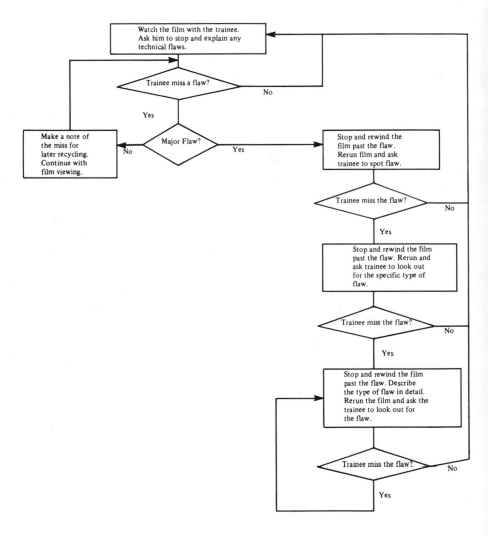

SIVASAILAM ("Thiagi") THIAGARAJAN began his career in education in Madras, India where he taught high school physics and math for six years. His home-grown instructional innovations attracted the attention of Dr. Douglas Ellson who invited him to come to the United States and work for him. Thiagarajan received his Ph.D. in Instructional Systems Technology from Indiana University. His professional experiences in the United States include administering six major instructional developmental projects, consulting with 40 organizations, serving on the editorial board of six professional journals, participating in national and international advisory panels and conducting more than 60 workshops all over the country. Thiagarajan has published six books and more than 40 articles on different aspects of instructional and performance technology and has produced 30 audiovisual training modules and 15 simulations/games.